Writing RFPs for Acquisitions

A GUIDE TO THE REQUEST FOR PROPOSAL

FRANCES C. WILKINSON

LINDA K. LEWIS

Acquisitions Section
Association for
Library Collections &
Technical Services

AMERICAN LIBRARY ASSOCIATION

Chicago   2008

ALCTS Acquisitions Guides

Guide to Licensing and Acquiring Electronic Information, #13
Stephen Bosch et al., 112p. 2005, Scarecrow Press.
ISBN: 0-8108-5259-4

Guide to Out-of-Print Materials, #12
Narda Tafuri et al., 46p. 2004, Scarecrow Press.
ISBN: 0-8108-4132-0

Guide to Managing Approval Plans, #11
Susan Flood, 58p. 1998, ALA.
ISBN: 0-8389-3481-1

Guide to Performace Evaluation of Serials Vendors, #10
38p. 1997, ALA.
ISBN: 0-8389-3469-2

*Guide to Selecting and Acquiring CD-ROMs, Software, and
other Electronic Publications,* #09
Stephen Bosch et al., 48p. 1994, ALA.
ISBN: 0-8389-0629-X

Guide to Preservation in Acquisition Processing, #08
Marsha J. Hamilton, 34p. 1993, ALA.
ISBN: 0-8389-0611-7

Guidelines for Handling Library Orders for Serials and Periodicals,
2d ed., #07
19p. 1992, ALA.
ISBN: 0-8389-3416-1

Statistics for Managing Library Acquisitions, #06
Eileen D. Hardy, 11p. 1989, ALA.
ISBN: 0-8389-3374-2

Guide to Performace Evaluation of Library Materials Vendors, #05
20p. 1988, ALA.
ISBN: 0-8389-3369-6

*Guidelines for Handling Library Orders for In-Print Monographic
Publications,* 2d Ed, #04
Sara C. Heitshu, 21p. 1984, ALA.
ISBN: 0-8389-3148-0

Guidelines for Handling Library Orders for Microforms, #03
  Harriet Rebuldela, 14p. 1977, ALA.
  ISBN: 0-8389-3193-6

*Guidelines for Handling Library Orders for Serials and
  Periodicals,* #02
  Murray S. Martin, 16p. 1974, ALA.
  ISBN: 0-8389-3158-8

*Guidelines for Handling Library Orders for In-Print Monographic
  Publications,* #01
  Murray S. Martin, 10p. 1973, ALA.
  ISBN: 0-8389-3148-0

ALCTS Publishing
50 E. Huron St.
Chicago, IL 60611
www.ala.org/alcts

ISBN: 978-0-8389-8483-3

Library of Congress Cataloging-in-Publication Data

Wilkinson, Frances C.
  Writing RFPs for acquisitions : a guide to the request for proposal / Frances C. Wilkinson, Linda K. Lewis.
     p. cm. -- (ALCTS acquisitions guides ; no. 14)
  Includes bibliographical references.
  ISBN 978-0-8389-8483-3
  1. Acquisitions (Libraries)--United States. 2. Library materials--Acquisition. 3. Books--Purchasing--United States. 4. Library fittings and supplies--Purchasing--United States. 5. Requests for proposals (Public contracts)--United States. I. Lewis, Linda K. II. Title.

  Z689.5.U6W56 2008
  025.20973--dc22
                        2008032559

Published and printed in the United States of America.

12 11 10 09 −08− 1 2 3 4

CONTENTS

CHAPTER **THREE**

Writing   20

APPENDIXES

CHAPTER ONE

Overview and Introduction

The first time you learn that you must prepare an RFP, or request for proposal, your reactions may include confusion, fear, irritation, frustration, or even anger, but it is very likely that your day will come. RFPs are used for many purposes, from construction to serials subscription management.

You may not know what an RFP consists of, much less how to prepare one, but you may have heard colleagues complain that their RFPs took incredible amounts of time and effort. You may believe that you will do all the preparation work, only to award the contract in the end to the company you have already identified as the best vendor. You may know that the purchasing and legal offices at your institution have many requirements for RFPs, but how do you go about finding out how they affect you and how to meet them? Few librarians have any training in preparing these documents, and these initial reactions are legitimate.

In spite of all these concerns, you *can* do a successful RFP in a reasonable amount of time and even use the RFP to improve your library's operations in important ways. To do so, you must plan and organize the process carefully. This guide presents the steps required to develop an RFP that will help you to assess library needs and plan, write, evaluate, and award a contract. It also suggests ways to implement and follow up on a contract and conduct a vendor evaluation.

An Overview

Libraries use vendors to acquire books, serials, databases, and media in various formats. The relationship between libraries and vendors has evolved over the years, but libraries and vendors remain dependent on each other. Only through the combined efforts of the vendor and the library can they both progress toward their respective goals of providing appropriate, quality materials to library users at a reasonable price. In the best situations, vendors can function as extensions of the library's staff, saving the library both time and money.

Libraries may conduct RFPs to select a wide range of products and services, for example:

■ Suppliers of books, journals, and databases

■ Suppliers of specialized materials, such as foreign language materials or media

■ Binders

■ Products for online use, such as integrated library systems or electronic resource management systems

■ Cataloging services

■ Construction

■ Equipment

This guide focuses on RFPs for the acquisition of books and journals, regardless of format, and databases.

Traditionally, libraries have selected vendors in a variety of ways, including the following:

■ Recommendations by colleagues

■ Relationships built gradually through visits and meetings at conferences

■ Personal preferences of someone on the library staff

Such methods are often effective, but the possibility of personal bias is high. You may have heard of cases where a library selected a vendor only because the director or some other person in the institution was a friend of the vendor's sales representative. In other cases, a vendor may be unfairly excluded from consideration as the result of a problem that occurred in the past but is no longer significant.

To minimize the effects of personal preference, many states require state agencies, including libraries, to adhere to procurement codes when purchasing goods and/or services that exceed a specified dollar amount. These codes attempt to ensure impartial competition, as well as to offer more opportunity for local businesses, including minority businesses, to compete.

What is Competitive Procurement?

Competitive procurement offers all vendors an equal opportunity to submit a proposal describing their capability to supply a good or service, such as library materials. It is used when multiple vendors are available to provide similar goods such as books or journals or services such as an approval plan. Competitive procurement stands in contrast to "sole source" procurement, which is used when there is only one way to obtain a product, such as the purchase of a manuscript from its owner. In the competitive procurement process, the rules and requirements are the same for all vendors, with no vendor offered special or unfair advantage.

The tools of competitive procurement are the request for information (RFI), request for quote (RFQ), or request for proposal (RFP), the subject of this guide. These processes are related, but each requests a slightly different response from the vendors.

This guide describes the RFP process, but it is useful here to describe the related documents, for contrast. The RFI is a request for information from a vendor regarding its available goods and services. An RFI is less specific than an RFP, because it asks for broad information rather than specific products or services. RFIs are often valuable to a library that is trying to determine what it requires and what is available in the marketplace *prior* to writing an RFP.

The RFQ is a request for quotation, quite specific, and often referred to as a *bid*. The award is given to the vendor that submits the lowest price, for example, highest discount or lowest service charge. Other factors such as customer service are not ranked high, if they are considered at all. Libraries may use an RFQ when price is the only, or at least the major, determining factor, so the RFQ is best suited to the purchase of specific goods, rather than services.

An RFP is most appropriate when a library knows what services or products are needed and when cost is only one of several factors in the selection. The RFP process allows a library to compare the vendor's history, customer services, and library offerings carefully.

What is an RFP?

The RFP is a development process as well as a document. As a process, it provides an objective method for a library to identify and clarify requirements, explore solutions, consider future directions, evaluate vendor proposals, select a vendor, and justify its decision. As a document, the RFP clearly articulates the library's requirements for vendor services, as well as instructions to vendors who wish to submit proposals. As both process and document, it uses the successful vendor's response as the basis for the contract, and the contract in turn as an instrument for the library to use in monitoring vendor compliance and performance throughout the contract period. RFPs can be used for virtually any product or service in a library including equipment or construction. This guide concentrates on the acquisition of library materials—print and electronic books, journals, and other library materials..

Advantages and Disadvantages of the RFP Process

Opponents and proponents of the RFP process abound in libraries. Both groups agree that reviewing an existing vendor's performance to determine whether new services are needed and what they are, evaluating several vendors' proposals, and then possibly implementing a change of vendors is hard work. Opponents of the

RFP process criticize the amount of time it requires. Having the a vendor continue supplying the same kinds of materials in the same ways in response to a plan or profile not revised for years does indeed release library staff for other work.

Further, opponents say that the RFP process seldom reveals anything that is not already known by the library. These opponents believe that if the library staff most directly involved with acquiring library materials would simply review the available information, they would rapidly and surely make the same decision that would take much longer to reach through an RFP process, and they argue that the RFP process wastes time and money that could be put to better use.

Supporters of the RFP process recognize that it is time-consuming but believe that it can be a valuable opportunity for the library to learn about new services and options. Even when a library and a vendor have worked closely together, the vendor's RFP response may include information that is new to the library. During the preparation for the RFP, library personnel will investigate many vendors and learn about new approaches and solutions. Because the process is competitive, vendors will present their best offers and libraries may be able to obtain better services or pricing than they would receive without going through it.

Proponents also believe that the RFP process minimizes bias and subjectivity. Vendors are evaluated equally against clear criteria established at the start of the process. While no process can be completely objective, the RFP process requires that everyone explain their rankings and their reasons. Adhering to this process greatly reduces personal bias.

Conclusion

The RFP process is indeed time-consuming and labor-intensive, both for the library and for the vendors who respond; however, the RFP is an extremely useful tool when prepared properly. It requires librarians to define their needs and determine how best to address them, reducing subjectivity and personal bias. An RFP allows librarians to compare products and services objectively and evaluate them realistically.

Librarians need the opportunity to fine-tune and evaluate what they buy and how they buy it. They must ensure that they receive the maximum value possible for each dollar that they expend. The RFP process can promote healthy competition among vendors, as well as help librarians to justify their decisions to others.

Librarians need an opportunity to learn what vendors have to offer, and the RFP process offers the structure and controls to ensure that they do. Although the process can take months to complete and still more months for the library to implement changes and to evaluate the results, the library is ultimately better for the effort.

CHAPTER TWO

Planning

This chapter provides guidelines for the following essential planning activities. Whether the RFP process is mandated by a governing body or voluntary on the part of the library, a well-organized and comprehensive plan will keep the process on track and on time throughout the planning, writing, and evaluation phases, which may take place over several months.

The recommendations in this chapter are directed primarily toward academic libraries, but they can be adapted easily to meet the needs of many public, school, special, and governmental libraries. Planning specifics will vary by library type.

The following activities are part of the planning phase:

- Construct a timeline
- Select a balanced task force or working group
- Meet with the library or institutional purchasing agent (researching institutional requirements regarding RFP requirements, regulations, and conduct of bidder relations)
- Select vendors to receive the RFP
- Arrange vendor on-site visits (optional)
- Write the RFP
- Evaluate vendor responses

■ Award the contract

■ Begin implementation

■ Review and evaluate vendor performance post-award

Constructing a Timeline

Establishing a timeline that will allow adequate time to complete each phase of the RFP process is perhaps the most important component of this phase. See appendix A for a sample timeline. The timeline must be a dynamic document, open to modification as needed, especially during initial meetings with the institution's purchasing agent and the RFP Task Force. The timeline should recognize the following phases:

Select the RFP Task Force. Once the Task force is selected, it should meet with the purchasing agent; hold discussions and conduct research (if needed) on library requirements; select the vendors to receive the RFP; and arrange on-site visits (if desired)

Write, review, and send the RFP. After drafting the RFP, make it available for review and comment by other library employees (if appropriate); send it to the purchasing agent for review; incorporate the purchasing agent's changes; decide on a date by which vendor responses are due; and send the RFP to the selected vendors.

Allow time for vendor response. Vendors should be given a specified number of days (typically thirty to forty-five days, depending upon local requirements and delivery time) to respond to the RFP. During this period, the RFP Task Force chair or designate answers any vendor questions (if appropriate and allowed by the purchasing department); The purchasing department receives all proposals, officially opens them, and forwards them to the library for review and selection

Evaluate the RFP and select a vendor. The RFP Task Force evaluates proposals, contacts vendor references, reviews and tabulates evaluation forms, discusses reference responses, and selects a vendor.

Formalize the selection and award the contract. The RFP Task Force provides recommendation, justification, and all supporting documentation and materials to the purchasing agent; the contract is awarded by purchasing department; and all vendors responding to the RFP are notified of the decision. There should also be a period set for vendor questions and challenges to the award. At the same time, the library can begin implementation.

The RFP process may take six months or more—thus it should be started well ahead of the intended start date for the implementation. Unexpected delays can occur in the library or the purchasing department. The Task force must remain flexible and consider each element of the timeline carefully to ensure that enough time is allowed to complete each step. For example, enough time must be allowed for vendors' references to be contacted; otherwise, the library could select a vendor that does not fulfill all of its requirements. If multiple libraries are involved, sufficient time must be allowed for each library to participate. If adequate time is not taken to meet all state or other regulations, the entire RFP could be invalidated. In many cases, the vendor must be given thirty days or more to respond to the RFP. These factors must be considered when establishing the timeline for the process.

Selecting an RFP Task Force

Most larger libraries will appoint an RFP Task Force to provide a balance of ideas and reduce potential bias in the process. Task force members should be drawn from the library units that are most directly involved in selecting and acquiring materials, including collection management and acquisitions and serials personnel. Other areas that may be included are electronic resources, cataloging, library fiscal services, and so on. Electronic resources personnel are vital to the task force if the RFP is to select a serials vendor, because the majority of academic print journals are also published electronically. Catalogers must be involved in the process if the RFP includes shelf-ready processing of materials. Library fiscal services staff may need to be part of the RFP Task Force; at any rate, they should be consulted about institutional policies and practices regarding invoicing and payment for materials. If bibliographic records will be downloaded to the library's online system, the managers of the Online Public Access Catalog (OPAC) should serve on, or advise, the Task force.

Members of the task force should possess good organizational, analytical, writing, and communication skills, because they will need to organize each step of the process, evaluate the vendor proposals, and communicate the reasons for their recommendation. The managers to whom the task force members report must understand that the RFP is a library priority and that the process is both rigorous and time-consuming. Task force members must have sufficient released time from their usual duties to participate in the RFP process.

Meeting with the Purchasing Agent

Early in the RFP process, the RFP Task Force chair, and other members of the task force if desired, must meet with the purchasing agent who is assigned to assist the library. This step is crucial when the task force chair is new to the RFP process or when the RFP is mandated and regulated by state law. At this initial meeting, the parties should be prepared to discuss the roles of the library and the purchasing agent. Each institution has its own requirements, and the task force must be aware of them before it begins to write the RFP to avoid potentially serious complications later. Here are some factors that frequently come up for consideration.

Contact with Vendors

It is important to clarify the type of contact that the library is authorized to have with vendors before sending the RFP, during the RFP response period, and immediately after the award. The following questions are a guide.

1. Can the library contact the vendor to obtain the contact information for the person to receive the RFP?
2. Can the library verify that the vendor company received the RFP, if it intends to respond, and whether it has responded?
3. Can the library answer vendors' questions about the RFP? Is communication restricted in any way during the RFP response period?
4. After receiving the vendor's response, can the library contact the vendor to clarify any part of the response? If not, does the purchasing agent perform these functions?

Purchasing Department Requirements for RFPs

RFP CONTENT

It is important to learn the purchasing department's requirements for the RFP document as a whole. The first part of the RFP document is the cover letter and administrative section; some institutions have a standard form or text (boilerplate) that must accompany all of their RFPs. See appendix A for a sample cover letter.

PROPOSAL PRESENTATION AND SCOPE

Other items to consider with the purchasing agent are the period of time that vendors have to respond to the RFP (typically thirty to forty-five days), the number of years that the contract will cover, and technical requirements regarding how the vendor's RFP response must be submitted (for example, paper or electronic document submission, number of paper copies, secure website submission, etc.).

INVITATIONS FOR LIBRARY VISITS

Some institutions require the library to invite all prospective vendors to make on-site presentations prior to the RFP. Others may allow the library to invite only the post-RFP finalists to give a presentation.

ROLE OF PRICE AND COST IN VENDOR EVALUATION

Ask whether the purchasing department requires that price or overall cost represent a specific percentage in the evaluation criteria, for example, a factor of 20 percent or more. Most public institutions will also include a disclaimer that the dollar value of the contract may change based on changes in the library's budget. Some institutions may give preference to local and/or minority businesses; the library will need to allow for that in its evaluation and scoring of the RFP responses.

RECEIPT OF VENDOR RESPONSES

Verify who will receive the vendor responses (typically, it is the purchasing agent) and how they will be delivered to the library for review. Must there be one task force member be designated to contact all vendor references or can various members contact those references? See appendix A for sample questions to ask of vendor references.

WHO HAS THE FINAL DECISION?

Finally, determine who is authorized to make the final decision to award the RFP and approve and sign the contract with the vendor. Is it the library director, the purchasing agent, the governing body of the parent institution, or someone else? The decision-making authority will vary depending on the type of organization, and it may also vary depending on the dollar value of the RFP. For example, some organizations require that any agreements or contracts with a dollar value over a specified amount must be reviewed and approved by the institution's legal office. Contracts with higher dollar values may require multiple levels of approval. Some universities may require that their CEO or governing board approve high-value contracts.

Selecting Vendors to Receive the RFP

Determine what kinds of vendors should receive the RFP. For example, if you are writing an RFP for standing orders, are you sending the RFP to approval plan vendors, serials vendors, or both? If you are preparing an RFP for acquiring scientific books, consider whether you will send it to a vendor that specializes in scientific and technical materials, a general vendor that handles them, or to both types of vendors.

To identify prospective vendors, especially specialty vendors for area studies, art books, children's books, etc., you can ask colleagues, consult electronic lists and professional associations, and visit exhibitors at conferences. Also, be sure to include vendors that you are working with now and those that have registered with your purchasing department to receive RFPs.

Even if the library or purchasing department has a vendor's contact information on file, you need to verify the current contact person and address for each vendor. At this time of numerous vendor mergers and personnel changes, this step is especially important to ensure that you have the correct contact information. If you send an RFP to a generic vendor address, it may not reach the person or unit that can handle the RFP response in a timely manner, if it reaches them at all.

Arranging Vendor Visits to the Library

Once the vendors are identified, consider whether you want to invite them to give an in-person presentation to your library staff about the services they offer. The library may also consider a vendor presentation by teleconference or conference call, as determined with the purchasing agent. If vendors are invited to the library, be sure to plan for an appropriate, technology-enabled space for the presentation. Have your technical support staff available to assist the vendors with the technology needed for their presentations to avoid technical difficulties. Coordinate the schedule so that the task force members and others who need to can attend. Treat all vendors equally; any appearance of favoritism may lead to challenges later, delaying the award or even invalidating the process and forcing the library to start over.

Planning to Write the RFP

When planning to write the RFP, do your homework carefully. Educate yourself about the RFP process through books, articles, and talking to or e-mailing colleagues who have recently gone through the process. Also, participate in online library discussion lists and attend an RFP workshop (perhaps at a conference) if time permits, to educate yourself. Your institution's purchasing department may offer workshops or maintain a web page that describes the steps and requirements of competitive procurement.

REVIEW YOUR PURPOSES

In the planning phase, the task force should discuss the purpose of the RFP. Why are you doing an RFP? Is there a problem with your existing vendor, or is the RFP being conducted only because it is a state or institutional requirement? What services do you really need? Have those circumstances changed since your last contract? This phase is your opportunity to get out of an acquisitions rut to discover new or improved vendor services, so take full advantage of the opportunity to educate both the task force and the library as a whole about vendors' services. Remember that library requirements must be stated clearly and succinctly in an RFP. If they are not, the vendors cannot respond properly, if they choose to respond at all.

CLARIFY YOUR QUESTIONS TO VENDORS

Craft questions to vendors carefully so that they understand what you are asking of them. For example, for approval plans, rather than asking "What is your discount?" ask the vendor to "Provide a complete list of your pricing, including all special charges," and ask whether charges will vary depending upon the size and mix of the library's account, and which of the options are available to your library. See appendix A for resources on model language for some kinds of questions.

CIRCULATE THE DRAFT RFP IN-HOUSE

Some libraries may wish to share the draft RFP with the library staff to solicit their comments and suggestions. This feedback will improve the quality and clarity of the RFP and increase the staff's understanding and buy-in to the process. Also, plan enough time for the purchasing agent to review the RFP and make changes.

CLARIFY PROPOSAL EVALUATION CRITERIA

Before writing the RFP, determine the criteria that will be used to evaluate the vendor responses to the RFP. You can then organize the requirements and questions the vendor must respond to around these criteria, making both the vendors' task and your own review of the responses easier. Ask your purchasing agent for any specific regulations that may apply.

CONSIDER PRICE VS. OVERALL COST CONSIDERATIONS

The factors used to evaluate vendors' responses will always include pricing; however, other factors such as company data, coverage, and customer service may be equally important to price, if not more important. *Price* is the amount assigned to the purchase of goods or services, less any discount and plus any service charge. *Overall cost considerations* may include value-added items that are not figured into the purchase price, such as providing rush orders without extra charges or offering a longer grace period on payments, as well as additional fees for services such as access to premium features in a vendor's database (for example, book reviews) or extra fees to receive approval plan slips in paper format.

ASSIGN RELATIVE IMPORTANCE TO THE EVALUATION CRITERIA

The RFP Task Force must determine which criteria to use and what percentage value will be assigned to each criterion, based on its relative importance. Some institutions may specify the percentage value assigned to overall cost considerations, for example, a minimum of 20 percent. Once the criteria are identified, an evaluation form must be planned and standardized. The form should allow ample space for each task force member to provide justification for the points they assign to each criterion. See appendix A for a sample vendor evaluation form.

Planning the RFP Evaluation

Once vendor responses to the RFP are received, the task force resumes its work. The plan must include enough time for the task force to evaluate the responses thoroughly, contact references, discuss the merits of each vendor response, and make a recommendation to the purchasing department. The following steps will ensure that these tasks are accomplished.

1. Assign a member of the task force to shepherd the vendor responses.
2. Identify a secure location for the task force members to review the RFP replies; replies are generally (and often legally) deemed confidential until an award is made.
3. Provide adequate space at the review location to spread out the documents provided by the vendor.
4. Make the evaluation forms readily available to task force members.
5. Send completed evaluation forms to the RFP Task Force chair (or a designee) to be tabulated.

The task force should agree in advance on consistent questions to be asked of the references supplied by each vendor. The following questions are examples. See appendix A for more sample questions.

- How long has the library worked with the vendor?
- What types of training does the vendor supply to the library staff?
- How effectively does the vendor resolve problems?

▨ How effective is the vendor's customer service?

▨ What is your experience with the vendor's online systems?

When the reference questions have been prepared, the task force should determine which members will contact the references and report their responses to the task force, if this process is not prescribed by the institution's purchasing department.

The task force should schedule a meeting to discuss the reports given by the vendor references and draft the recommendation. The task force chair will also need adequate time to consult with appropriate members of the library administration, and the purchasing agent if necessary, about the recommendation.

Planning to Award the RFP

Once the task force has agreed on a vendor, it must prepare a written recommendation for awarding the contract. Plan sufficient time for each step:

1. Who will write the letter of justification that summarizes the recommendation? This person is usually the task force chair.

2. Which library staff members have to approve the recommendation? Which persons or groups outside the library need to approve it? For example, the purchasing department or central administration (including the legal office or the governing board) may have approval authority.

3. Who is responsible for notifying all vendors that submitted a response?

4. In the event that the task force wants to hold discussions with two or three of the highest-ranked vendors after reviewing the responses, are such meetings permitted by local regulations and purchasing department policy?

5. Who responds to any vendor questions or challenges?

6. How many days do vendors have to challenge an award? The number of days a vendor has to challenge an award must be built into the timeline.

Finally, someone in the library, typically the RFP Task Force -chair, communicates the results of the process to the library. That person also provides the vendor contract to the library's administration and to the managers of acquisitions, serials, collection management and any other appropriate areas.

Planning Contract Implementation and Follow-up

If the contract is awarded to a new vendor, the library must work closely with both the previous and new vendors to plan for the transition. The transfer process invariably takes more time than expected. If the contract is for a new approval plan vendor, the library will need to create a profile with the new vendor. The previous vendor will have to be notified of the date to cease book shipments. If the contract is for a new serials vendor, all subscriptions will have to be transferred from the previous vendor to the new one. This process can be very involved, and clear communication is critical.

Conclusion

The successful outcome of an RFP depends on the initial planning. A lack of planning can result in a poorly worded RFP to which few, if any, vendors will respond. The vendors that do respond may not be able to respond adequately.

A carefully constructed timeline is essential. A well-balanced task force must be appointed. The chair of the task force must meet with the purchasing agent for the organization to clarify everyone's roles and responsibilities, as well as the legal requirements for the RFP document. All vendors including those identified by the library as well as those on file at the institution's purchasing department should receive the RFP, with adequate time to respond.The library may want to arrange on-site visits or teleconference with the vendors.

The RFP document must include a cover letter that succinctly describes both required and desired elements and clearly specifies the criteria by which the RFP will be evaluated. The evaluation process must be carefully planned, allowing enough time to read all responses thoroughly, call vendor references, discuss task force members' evaluations, and craft the justification letter. If a new vendor is selected, the library will have to develop a transition plan, as well as perform a follow-up and evaluation of the vendor who is awarded the contract.

The time spent in the planning phase lays the foundation for writing the RFP and clarifies the criteria to be used in the evaluation process. Some aspects of planning and writing the RFP may occur simultaneously, depending on the preference of the task force. The time invested in planning will be rewarded by better responses from the vendors and a more successful relationship with the vendor throughout the duration of the contract.

CHAPTER THREE

Writing

This chapter provides guidelines for writing an RFP that will serve multiple purposes. By the time writing begins, the content of each major section of the RFP should have been discussed and agreed upon, including the evaluation criteria. Some of the actual writing may have been developed in the planning phase as well.

The RFP should be structured to support the library in accomplishing the following tasks:

1. Inform vendors of exactly what the library is looking for
2. Provide vendors the opportunity to respond precisely to library requirements and budgets
3. Provide the library with criteria-based information on vendor capabilities
4. Evaluate the vendors' customer service responsiveness
5. Provide detailed information on overall cost considerations for doing business with
6. Form the basis for the contract to be awarded to the successful vendor
7. Evaluate post-award performance

At the time of writing, some of these events lie months ahead, but a well-written RFP document lays the groundwork for performing all of them. To work best, the document should elicit information that is detailed and thorough enough to be compared across various vendor responses. Writing the RFP document is not just putting pen to paper; it includes all of the following activities:

- Prepare the cover letter
- Establish the general requirements
- Address possible future requirements
- Build objective questions (about the company and its customer service and its approval plan, serials, or database capabilities)
- Capture overall cost considerations
- Develop vendor evaluation criteria

As the writing phase begins, the task force must consider a number of factors. The RFP document should be *S M A R T*—*S*pecific, *M*easurable, *A*chievable, *R*elevant, and Timebound. This acronym has been widely used in the literature of human resources management to describe criteria for setting performance goals, and it is equally useful in the RFP process. Here are some guidelines:

Include your timeline for implementation of the project.

Be specific about your requirements, distinguishing them clearly from desirable elements that are not crucial to the project.

Ask questions that will produce measurable responses, so that they can be answered and evaluated objectively.

Do not require services or products that are not achievable or are still in theoretical development.

Generally, if a vendor cannot supply a required element, you should eliminate the vendor from further consideration. Limit your questions to those that are relevant to the topic of your RFP. When developing questions, consider how you will objectively evaluate their answers.

If you need broad information about an area, you may need to begin with an RFI before you move to the RFP.

It is important to avoid jargon and phrases and terminology that are used primarily by one vendor—RFPs must be clear, avoid bias, and be written in impartial, non-discriminatory language. If you use any terms that are open to interpretation, they should be defined. Never assume that vendors will be able to guess accurately what you hope to see in their responses.

Keep the RFP document succinct, but be sure to include all essential aspects. Vendors must respond to the RFP and the task force must read and thoroughly evaluate each vendor's response. Ask both specific and open-ended questions to allow the vendors a place to describe their services and various options. For example, in addition to asking for specific information about costs or coverage, ask how services are provided and what additional services are available.

Consider having your RFP reviewed by a colleague who has recently participated in an RFP process. This feedback can identify omissions and areas that need clarification. If possible, have your RFP read by someone who does not work in the area involved with the subject of the RFP; this will help identify areas that are confusing or contain jargon.

Each section of the RFP should be clearly labeled. See appendix A for model language for an RFP. At minimum, these sections should be included: the cover letter, general requirements, overall cost considerations, and evaluation criteria. Work with your purchasing agent to determine the exact structure required by your institution.

Preparing the Cover Letter

The introduction to the RFP is referred to in different ways, sometimes as the cover letter or administrative section, other times as the instructions to vendors section. The terms used to describe the introductory information will vary by institution with some RFPs being divided into separate sections to handle each item. These sections may include a very brief cover letter that identifies only the institution and the nature of the RFP, a detailed description of the terms and conditions of the RFP, and a description of the institutions' legal requirements for submitting an RFP. Always consult your purchasing agent to determine your institutions' requirements. Regardless of the name used by the library or the purchasing department, this section contains the purpose of the RFP, for example, approval plan, serials, electronic databases, etc. It also includes background information about the library and its parent institution, or consortia of which it is a part. The description should include its clientele, programs, and the size and strength of its collections; operating budget; staff size; and appropriate information about its technical requirements, for example, its integrated library system, bibliographic utility, etc. See appendix A for a sample cover letter.

The cover letter should also include the proposal number; contact information for both the purchasing agent and the library's RFP Task Force chair or designate, with street and email addresses and phone and fax numbers; estimated value of the contract, along with a statement that the value is approximate based on the library's future budget allocation, and not a guaranteed amount; the time period covered by the contract; and grounds for termination of the contract.

The cover letter must also describe how vendor responses must be delivered (means, format, address, conformity to the legal requirements of the parent institution). Some details that should be included are the following:

- Number of copies of the proposal and any additional exhibits required
- Format for the response, for example, electronic, paper, or posting on a secure website
- Location where and date by which the response must be received
- Whether all responses will be held and officially opened only on the closing date, or opened as they are received or at some other point.
- General terms, conditions, and instructions to the vendor as required by the purchasing department.

Generally, the RFP response serves as the contract, but in some cases it is merely the basis for the negotiation and a separate contract is issued. The procedure for arriving at the final contract, including any negotiation period expected, should be spelled out.

In addition, the cover letter may include:

- Statements about the institutional policy on minority and/or small business preference
- Reservation of the right to split the award among two or more vendors, and the right not to make an award at all if no satisfactory response is received.
- Cancellations, changes, and alterations after the award
- Conflict of interest clauses
- Indemnification and insurance
- Equal opportunity and affirmative action statements.

In addition, each vendor should be instructed to provide a minimum of three references. Ask that these references be libraries comparable in size and type to your library, and that at least one of the references be a library that recently transferred its account to the vendor. Contacting this reference will provide an indication of how well the vendor handles the account transfer process. Also, ask that at least one of the references use the same integrated library system as your library. The reference will give you some insight into how well the vendor's system interfaces with the library system you use.

Establishing the General Requirements

The general requirements section outlines what the library is purchasing from the vendor and then describes in detail the specific materials or services. The statement of requirements is usually relatively small and contains only those core elements that the vendor must provide to remain in consideration.

Here are some questions that might be addressed in this section.

Is the library seeking a vendor to provide books for an approval plan, or does it plan to place firm orders for specific titles?

Is the library looking for a vendor who can provide electronic books as part of the approval profile?

For an RFP for an approval plan, what is the range of the vendor's subject, geographic, and language coverage, and what are their online systems and services?

Is the library is looking for a vendor that specializes in art exhibition catalogs, music scores, media, scientific/technical journals, or area studies journals?

Is the library looking for a vendor to handle its domestic, foreign, or both types of serial subscriptions?

If you are doing an RFP for serials, what are the specific services provided by the vendor in association with electronic journals?

Addressing Possible Future Requirements

Contracts are awarded for several years. While libraries must focus first and foremost on what they require today, for example shelf-ready cataloging, they must also consider what they may want tomorrow. Therefore, the library may wish to leave the option for the vendor to provide information on its future plans for new products and services. Accurate predictions are nearly impossible, given the speed of change; however, the task force should review developing technology and remain open to alternative approaches. If the library is considering major changes in staffing levels or other areas, such as plans to change its integrated library system during the contract period, the task force should inform the vendor. The task force must also consider what impact these potential changes may have on the vendors' responses and the RFP implementation.

Building Objective Questions

Ask questions in a way that allows answers to be evaluated objectively. Avoid asking the vendors yes-or-no questions. Instead, ask open-ended questions that allow the vendors to describe their services and explain the options they can offer. However, remember that the vendor must respond to all the questions contained in the RFP, and the library must evaluate all answers—however open-ended they may be, questions must be both relevant and meaningful to the library.

Questions About the Company

The questions that you will ask the vendors depend on the type of RFP you are writing; however, there are questions suitable for all types of RFPs, such as information about the vendor company and its electronic or computer-based services and customer service.

Company data questions should elicit information about the background and stability of the company. Questions may include:

- How long the company has been in business?
- How many offices does it have? Which office would handle the library's account?
- How many libraries similar to yours does it serve?
- What is the size of the vendor's staff and what are their qualifications and training?
- What is the vendor's financial condition?

For public companies, you can request a statement of financial condition and a copy of the annual report. You can also research the company background independently, using business and financial reference tools. Some vendors that provide financial documents may request that the information be kept confidential and be provided only to members of the task force. Some may even require the institution to sign a non-disclosure agreement to ensure that their financial information does not become public.

Questions to Assess Electronic Capabilities and Services

Electronic or computer-based services continue to develop rapidly. Libraries now routinely require vendors to provide electronic systems, interfaces, services, and capabilities. Areas to consider may include ease of use and special features of the vendor's system such as interfaces with the library's system, bibliographic utilities, or other electronic products. Most vendors now provide electronic ordering, claims, cancellation, and invoicing. Many provide cataloging, processing, and a host of other services. The methods of delivering these services vary among vendors, and the library will want to consider which services are required and which features are preferences. Vendors are developing new products and services rapidly, so you should ask questions that allow the vendors to describe what products and services are currently available, as well as what they anticipate developing.

Questions to Assess Customer Service

Another element that should be addressed in all types of RFPs is customer service. Customer service is of great importance to the library, and its value should not be underestimated. Good customer service creates satisfaction and loyalty, whereas poor customer service will eventually cost the vendor the library's account. Libraries want knowledgeable, service-oriented vendor staff who are readily available and who resolve problems promptly. The customer service representatives of the company keep the library informed about new vendor products and services, trends in the market, and upgrades and improvements in the vendors' systems.

Because of the importance of quality customer service, the library will want to craft its desired elements carefully to get the best understanding possible of how the vendor views its customer-service role. How long will it take a customer service representative to respond to a question or problem from the library? Will a specific representative be assigned to the library's account? If the library transfers its account to the vendor, what services will be available to facilitate the transfer?

Questions for Approval Plan Vendors

Specific questions will depend upon the type of the RFP. If you are conducting an RFP for an approval plan vendor, your questions might include the following:

- How does the vendor select and analyze books?

- How is the profile created?
- What types of materials does the vendor exclude, for example, foreign language, government, media, etc.?
- What return rate is anticipated?
- How will the library's profile be updated?
- Is there is a limit on the number of times the profile can be revised in a given period?
- What type of records does the vendor provide?
- What type of database does the vendor provide and what are its features?

Questions for Serials Vendors

If you are conducting an RFP for a serials vendor your questions might include:

- How does the vendor handle electronic packages of journals and/or databases?
- How does the vendor handle claims for print journal issues?
- What kind of management reports are available and can they be easily tailored to fit the library's specifications?
- What are the deadlines for cancellations?
- What types of materials does the vendor exclude, for example, government publications?

Questions for Database Vendors

If you know that you want a specific database that is available from multiple sources, the questions you ask in the RFP will include the cost, the interface used, and the customer service provided for the database. Specific questions might also include:

- How frequently is the database updated?
- What technical support does the vendor provide?
- How is the cost determined?

If you are looking for a database that covers a wide range of subjects and journals, you need to ask more questions in the RFP, some broader and some more detailed. They might include the following:

- What subjects are covered in the database?
- How frequently are the subject areas or sections of interest updated?
- How is the cost determined?
- Can the library tailor the appearance of the database, for example, can the library specify whether the default screen is the basic search page or the advanced search page?
- How are usage statistics monitored and reported?

The library may also ask for samples of profiling tools, invoices, order and cancellation acknowledgments, management reports, and trial access to the vendor's systems; most vendors have test databases available. Some will provide temporary passwords to the complete database, allowing sufficient access for library staff to evaluate the system.

Capturing Overall Cost Considerations

Pricing information in itself is a fairly straightforward section of the RFP. Most book vendors offer a discount on the list price of individual titles, and most serials vendors add an additional service charge to the subscription price. Generally, the higher the discount for books and the lower the service charge for serials, the better.

However, overall cost considerations do not stop with discounts and service charges. Here are some questions to ask to elicit more information.

- Are there cost reductions available that are based on the dollar value of the account or the type of materials supplied?
- Is there a prepayment discount? If so, what is the amount and when must prepayment be received? There may be more than one option.

- Will the vendor provide a complete list of charges for all possible value-added services, such as rush shipping and handling and enhanced bibliographic records?
- What is the timeframe for payment? Are late fees assessed?
- For foreign vendors, will the library be billed in U.S. dollars? If not, how will the conversion and exchange rate be handled? The library may wish to require an additional grace period for payment, or billing in U.S. dollars only.

Pricing for databases is less straightforward and is frequently negotiated based on a library's budget or enrollment size.

Developing Vendor Evaluation Criteria

The RFP Task Force must develop an evaluation form, containing the various point-weighted criteria for each factor of the RFP. See appendix A for a sample vendor evaluation form. Typically, the criteria for evaluating the RFP responses are set when the RFP is in the planning and writing stages and usually in consultation with the purchasing agent. The RFP should define the criteria clearly, reflecting the value that the library places on each section of the request; and it should be made clear to vendors that the criteria will be used to evaluate their responses.

Evaluation factors will vary by the type of RFP, but generally include company data, coverage provided, electronic or computer-based services, customer service, overall cost considerations, as well as the areas that are unique to the type of RFP. The RFP Task Force should adhere to the evaluation factors. Members should keep the library's priorities and needs in mind and should not let themselves be swayed by additional features or services that the library does not need or plan to use.

Although price is important, most libraries give more weight to customer service. However, some institutions require that a minimum percentage be assigned to overall cost considerations, often 20 percent or some higher number. The weight given to other factors, such as electronic or computer-based services, varies by library. To simplify the weighting process, it may help to make the total points or percentages add up to 100 or some other normative total.

Conclusion

A concise, well-written RFP lays the foundation for a successful outcome; a poorly worded RFP will result in frustration for both the library and the vendors. RFPs should be written SMART, so that they are Specific, Measurable, Achievable, Relevant, and Timebound. They must be written clearly in impartial, non-discriminatory language that is free of jargon and terms that are used by only one vendor. The questions should facilitate both the vendors' responses and the library's evaluation (each vendor's response must be read and evaluated). Each section of the RFP should be clearly labeled, and each criterion to be used in the evaluation should be stated, along with additional questions that will encourage vendors to provide adequate, measurable information for the evaluation and award process. The RFP and vendor response typically constitute the contract itself and set the tone for the library-vendor business relationship. Time spent in writing the RFP will be repaid with a solid foundation for implementation and for future relationship between the library and the vendor.

CHAPTER FOUR

Evaluating Proposals and Awarding the Contract

This chapter provides guidelines for the activities that must take place once vendor proposals are received. Only the last item, managing challenges from unsuccessful vendors, may be ongoing, but the plan for managing challenges must be in place before the award is announced.

The main activities during the evaluation and award phase are the following:

1. Review vendor proposals against the library evaluation criteria published in the RFP
2. Contact libraries served by the vendor for references on the vendor's performance
3. Elicit task force evaluations of the vendor proposals
4. Bring the task force to agreement on which vendor to recommend
5. Prepare a justification letter to support the vendor selection
6. Notify vendors of the contract award
7. Manage challenges from unsuccessful vendors (this activity may be ongoing)

Once the deadline for vendors to respond to the RFP has passed, the purchasing agent officially opens the replies and forwards them to the library for review by the RFP Task Force. The task force must consider each response carefully and fully because the library will have to justify its recommendation and live with its decision for several years. After months spent in planning for and writing the RFP, the task force may be tempted to rush the evaluation process to reach a conclusion and make the award, but doing so may well result in overlooking critical details. Mistakes in the evaluation process can result not only in the contract being awarded to a vendor that cannot provide the products or services needed by the library, but also in an appeal by unsuccessful vendors. If the appeal is upheld, the award will be invalidated and the RFP process will have to be repeated.

Reviewing Proposals Against Evaluation Criteria

If the RFP has been written with clear, considered, and measurable vendor questions and statements of the library requirements, the evaluation process should not be overwhelming. In some institutions, the purchasing agent may perform a quick review to determine that all vendors replying to the RFP are capable of meeting the requirements stated by the library.

It may happen that a vendor submits an incomplete RFP is submitted, lacking either sufficient depth of information or answers to one or more questions. Institutional practices regarding such RFPs vary; the purchasing agent can consult with the task force to determine whether incomplete responses are to be barred and removed from further consideration or are to be evaluated but ranked lower because of the missing elements. If a preliminary review is not performed by the institution's purchasing agent before the responses are sent to the library for review, the RFP Task Force should perform a cursory review of each submittal before evaluations begin, to verify that all required elements are met. If they are not, the response may be debarred.

The next step is for each RFP Task Force member to review each vendor's response carefully, including scrutiny of all samples and appendices. If a the vendor has provided trial access to its database or online system, RFP Task Force members, and others if appropriate and authorized, must evaluate the system as part of the process. Computer services are increasingly vital elements of vendors' products and services.

In most cases, only the task force members are allowed to review the RFP responses. Confidentiality is crucial to the integrity of the RFP evaluation process, and in some cases, libraries may have to sign a non-disclosure document to cover the information gathered through an RFP. No information obtained as a result of the vendor review can be shared with others inside the library or external to it, especially vendor financial data. Just as you expect vendors to respect the confidentiality of information you provide in an RFP, you must respect the confidentiality of vendor responses.

The standardized form used for evaluation should focus on the point-weighted criteria that were put forth in the RFP. Numerical scales are easiest to document, especially if there is a challenge. You may decide to assign a range of points or percentages to help you evaluate the main criteria. For example, if company data comprises 10 percent of the total score, you can use a range of 0 percent to 10 percent to score that category. See appendix A for a sample vendor evaluation form.

Each task force member must evaluate each vendor's response and explain the point values they assigned to each vendor for each criterion. Asking evaluators to explain their rankings helps to keep everyone objective and provides the information needed to write the justification for the award. The evaluation form should allow space for comments about each criterion and a comment on the overall ranking.

Libraries can perform the evaluations by reviewing paper forms or using online project management or other collaborative software, or a shared local area drive where all task force members can review the vendor response forms and post their input. Access to the files must be restricted to the RFP Task Force members, with password protection. Check with your systems group and your purchasing agent to determine whether online collaborative review is possible and acceptable at your institution.

Institutions sometimes place additional constraints on the evaluations of response to RFPs, and these constraints should be considered in advance. The task force should be aware that evaluations may be reviewed by others in the parent organization— and by vendors, especially in cases where the award is later challenged by an unsuccessful vendor. The institution may require that all the evaluation forms be sent to the purchasing agent with the final recommendation is submitted, and some institutions may eliminate all the evaluations done by a task force member who has not evaluated every vendor.

Contacting Vendor References

Next, RFP Task Force members must carefully check each vendor reference. Obviously, vendors are not going to provide the names of dissatisfied customers, so critical questioning is necessary to elicit meaningful responses. Libraries may ask questions about the vendor's customer services or computer systems, what the vendor does well, and what types of training and support the vendor provides. See appendix A for sample questions to address to vendor references.

Vendor references will provide information about how the vendor actually interacts with its clients, how they respond to problems, and how well their systems function. Tell the references that the information they provide will provide background information for the library's recommendation but that their confidentiality will be maintained to the extent legally possible.

To ensure fairness, ask each vendor reference the same questions, but follow up with specific, probing questions when necessary— answers to these questions can be even more enlightening than answers to the initial question. When asking about customer service, for example, encourage the references to discuss the types of problems that occurred and how they were resolved. Follow-up questions could include asking about the amount of time needed to resolve problems or the extent and quality of communication during the process.

The library can conduct reference interviews either by phone or via email. There are advantages and disadvantages to each method. Phone reference contacts have to be scheduled at times convenient for both task force members and the person giving the reference. The task force member may wish to e-mail the questions to the references prior to the telephone interview allow them to prepare and gather any needed information. Answers must be accurately recorded in writing or by other means and then transcribed, because it may be necessary to send the transcripts to the purchasing agent along with the final recommendation. Telephone calls allow you to ask immediate, probing questions. The respondent may reveal information through voice tone and inflection, but it is difficult to document those factors thoroughly in a transcript.

Contact with references may be e-mail, and references may be asked to reply in the same way. E-mailing the vendor performance questions allows the reference to answer them at their convenience and to respond more fully—they can look up or verify information before answering or consult with others in the organization who may have more experience with the vendor or provide additional information. With a written response, everything is laid out clearly, unlike what happens when an interviewer takes notes during a phone call. Further, no transcription is necessary; e-mail responses can be forwarded or printed and included in the information forwarded to the purchasing agent. When e-mail responses require clarification, the task force member conducting the interview may either ask the follow-up questions via email or call the reference for a follow-up discussion.

Completing the Vendor Evaluation Forms

During this activity, task force members record their individual evaluations of each proposal, using a form that mirrors the evaluation criteria spelled out in the RFP. See appendix A for a sample vendor evaluation form.

Agreeing on the Recommendation

After RFP Task Force members have contacted vendor references and completed their evaluation forms, the forms are tabulated and the task force meets to discuss its recommendation. The meeting can take place in person, or task force members may deliberate in a teleconference or use a collaboration software program. Some libraries use collaboration software to conduct most of the RFP process, especially if the RFP is designed to serve a multi-site system or consortia whose members are at a distance from each other.

Task force members may have significant differences of opinion about which vendor should receive the award. Members may need to re-read sections of the vendor responses to compare or confirm answers. One member of the task force may discover something in the responses that others missed. Depending upon local regulations and the policy of the purchasing department, the task force may want to contact a vendor to clarify a response, or even bring the highest-ranked vendors in for an on-site presentation. If vendors have already made presentations regarding the RFP, the two or three highest-ranked vendors may be invited for a second visit.

Preparing and Submitting the Justification Letter

Once the RFP Task Force has agreed upon the recommendation, it prepares a justification letter to summarize the entire process and document the decision reached by the task force and the library. This document is will prove to the purchasing agent and the parent institution that the library has reached a valid decision, and it must document that the library has adhered to all the institutions' policies and procedures when conducting the RFP process.

The justification letter includes the names of the RFP Task Force members, the names of the vendors responding, the criteria used to rank the responses, and the points assigned to each vendor in each of the criteria. In addition, the letter summarizes the strengths and weaknesses of each vendor and explains why the task force recommends one vendor over the others. It summarizes the comments of the references, but generally does not identify individual names or institutions.

When writing the justification, use neutral, non-prejudicial terms to describe your concerns, for example, the term *discrepancy* instead of *error*. When possible, use quotes from the vendor's response rather than rewording their statements. The clearer and more straight-forward the justification, the less likely it is that the decision will be challenged by either the purchasing agent or another vendor. See appendix A for a sample of a letter of justification.

Typically, the recommendation is reviewed by the director of the library, who may choose to meet with the entire RFP Task Force or its chair to discuss it. After the library director approves the recommendation, the letter and accompanying information are forwarded to the purchasing agent for review. The purchasing agent may also wish to meet with the RFP Task Force chair to clarify any questions.

Accompanying the letter of justification should be a summary of task force members' comments and a composite of their evaluation scores. In some cases, the original evaluation forms completed by each task force member for each vendor will be required. Copies of e-mails exchanged with the vendors' references and transcripts of telephone conversations, should accompany the justification letter.

In some cases, the library's letter of justification is provided to all vendors, including those who bid unsuccessfully, and the letter should be written with that distribution in mind. Even when the letter is not provided to all vendors, some may request it. You must be fair, accurate, and thorough in your explanations.

Notifying Vendors

Once the decision has been made, the purchasing agent usually issues an official letter of notification to the vendors; however, sometimes the library contacts the vendors. It is important to clarify the notification process and the roles of the library and the purchasing agent early in the planning process.

Even when the purchasing agent notifies the vendors, it is sometimes professionally appropriate if the library follows-up by communicating directly with them, both the successful vendor and those not selected. Just because a vendor did not receive a given award, they may win the award in the future and the library may do other business with them at any time. Courteous, professional communications will always serve the library well.

Further, an unsuccessful vendor may wish to ask the library directly why they were not awarded the contract and how the company could improve its response in the future. It is important to clarify with the purchasing agent what information can be shared with the competing vendors. Unsuccessful vendors will carefully scrutinize the award justifications and could even challenge the award if the justifications are not clear and accurate.

Managing Challenges to the Award

Unsuccessful vendors have the right to challenge any award they believe was made unfairly. Although these challenges are rare and even more rarely successful if the RFP process was well planned, you need to be aware of the possibility. You must know who handles the response to the challenge. In most cases, it will be handled by several people, including the purchasing agent, the RFP chair or designate, and the institution's legal counsel.

When this group meets to plan the response to the challenge, its first step will be to review the vendor's reasons for challenging the decision. The RFP chair should provide the files of the task force's activities, notes, and recommendation. Detailed documentation of each phase of the process is critical to proving that the process was managed in full compliance with the institutional policy and governing regulations or laws. Confidentiality is vital during defense of any challenge to the award.

Conclusion

Evaluation of the vendor proposals is a crucial phase in the RFP process. Although it may be tempting to rush through the evaluation to make a recommendation and award the contract, rushing can create many problems. The library may miss vital information, selecting an inappropriate vendor or opening the door to a challenge of the award. Sufficient time must be allocated for the RFP Task Force to review each vendor's response carefully, and the justification letter must then be crafted carefully to present the recommendations clearly. The evaluation process must be thorough and impartial, and the analysis must be fully documented to identify the vendor that can best meet the needs of the library.

CHAPTER FIVE

Implementation, Follow-Up, and Vendor Evaluation

This chapter provides guidelines for the post-award components of the process, which include the following:

■ Implementing the contract (for both approval plans and serials)

■ Performing a post-award follow-up with the vendor

■ Procedures for evaluating vendor performance

Implementing the Contract

Once the contract has been awarded, the library begins the contract implementation. Like planning the RFP process, evaluating vendor responses, and justifying vendor selection, the contract implementation and follow-up require the library to plan appropriately, with great attention to detail.

In most cases, the vendor's response and the institution's award letter constitute the contract between the vendor and the institution. Occasionally, the institution will create a separate contract summarizing all aspects of the agreement.

As you begin implementation, review and compile all the files to bring together all aspects of the agreement. Having one consolidated package will simplify monitoring and evaluation throughout the contract. Keep copies of all pertinent documentation. You will need these during the transfer phase if you are switching vendors, to monitor and evaluate vendor performance during the life of the contract, and as a model for the next time the library conducts an RFP.

Typically, the purchasing department keeps copies of all documentation from the vendors submitting a response, and the library department conducting the RFP will keep copies of all vendor documentation until enough time has passed to ensure that the award will not be challenged by other vendors. Multiple copies of the successful vendor's proposal and award should be kept at the library: one in the department that oversees the implementation and ongoing vendor evaluation, and one in the library director's administrative office.

If the contract award goes to the current vendor, little work is required on the part of the library apart from acquainting library personnel with the changes negotiated in the new contract. If the library is changing approval plan vendors, serials vendors, database vendors, or others, it must allocate sufficient time and staff resources to the transition. It must determine how the transfer will be handled, which materials will be transferred, and what kinds of follow-up activities will make the process as smooth as possible.

Approval Plans

Changing approval plan vendors involves several library groups. Collection development librarians will create the new profile. Acquisitions staff will set procedures for receiving and paying for the materials. The systems or cataloging staff must decide how to manage the bibliographic records transmitted to the library's integrated library system by the vendor. Timing of the transfer of approval plans is crucial; library staff must work with the previous and new vendors to set an exact date for the former to stop providing books and the latter to start doing so. In addition, if the vendor's response included a discount factor based on the mix of books to be provided, the library must plan to negotiate the final discount after the profile is complete. The library must also decide whether this final negotiation is to be managed by the RFP Task Force chair, the library director, or the purchasing agent.

Serials

Transferring serials titles, whether under paper or electronic subscriptions , often requires more time and effort than expected. The library must establish a date for subscriptions to be taken over by the new vendor. The transition for journals generally works well on a calendar-year subscription basis, but serials with irregular publications schedules will be more challenging. For example, the previous vendor's cancellation notice to the publisher or distributor may cross the new vendor's order for the same serial publication, thus confusing the publisher. The library may receive two copies of a title, or none at all. If some titles are supplied as part of a membership, the library must verify that the new vendor has identified each title included in the membership package and that those titles are transferred accordingly. Missing issues, interrupted service, increased numbers of claims, payment problems, and binding problems can be costly in terms of staff time and funds and will certainly be aggravating to library users. To avoid this kind of confusion, the library must take time to work closely with both vendors, but the time taken will pay off over the life of the contract.

When transferring databases to a new vendor, the library has to provide its Internet Protocol (IP) addresses to the vendor and obtain the Web addresses that library patrons will need to use the databases. In some cases, new licensing agreements will have to be negotiated and signed. With the new vendor, the database interface and search capabilities may be somewhat different, and both your staff and your customers must be trained to use the new interface efficiently. Reference and instruction personnel must learn to use the new resource before they begin helping library patrons to use it. Some vendors may provide access for staff training for a short time before the official subscription begins; it is wise to ask the vendor if this is an option.

Performing the Initial Follow-up

The library is required both legally and professionally to expend its acquisitions budget wisely and efficiently, and it must ensure that the vendor honors the conditions of the contract, delivering what it agreed to, in the way it agreed to, and at the price it specified. Monitoring the contract from the beginning is crucial; otherwise, the library may forfeit the ability to enforce the terms later.

Although formal vendor performance evaluation usually begins several months into the contract when there is enough data to evaluate, early detection and resolution of minor problems can prevent major problems from occurring later. For example, approval plan profiles often need minor adjustments to improve coverage or exclude unwanted books. Correcting such minor adjustments is a much better strategy than allowing problems to grow until a major revision of the profile is necessary or it becomes very difficult to identify what materials were not supplied. If serial titles transferred to a new vendor do not start with the expected issues, the library must claim the missed issues quickly to avoid gaps in the collection. If access to databases does not start on the anticipated date, users will be inconvenienced. It is important to document all problems and work with the vendor to resolve issues as soon as possible.

Evaluating Vendor Performance Post-Award

There is a great variety in the way libraries evaluate vendor performance, ranging from simple one-factor studies to complex data analyses. Libraries should review the extensive body of literature on vendor evaluation to identify which methods may be most appropriate. Both the vendor's management reports and data obtained from library systems are useful tools. The library should allow enough time to monitor and collect data on vendor performance, typically ranging from a few months to a maximum of a year. The vendor evaluation will either confirm or call into question the staff's initial perceptions, but it is important to be objective. Any transfer process will have some initial problems, and there also be some staff resistance and resentment toward a new vendor. A formal evaluation will be more reliable than personal impressions.

The library must first determine which aspects of vendor performance it wants to evaluate. Staff members will usually have a sense of some problem areas, and their impressions can be useful in identifying areas needing systematic evaluation. The following questions may come up, among others.

1. Does the library want to determine if the vendor is consistently applying the correct discounts on its approval plan or the correct service charge on its serials?
2. Is the library monitoring database downtime? What baseline has been set?
3. Is the library trying to determine rejection rate percentages on its approval plan?
4. Is the library tracking customer service response time?

The next step is to determine what will be evaluated, when the evaluation will begin and its duration, and the method to be used. The goal of the evaluation is to determine whether the vendor is meeting the library's expectations and to identify any areas that need to be adjusted.

Some possible factors to be evaluated are:

1. Accuracy of the vendor's management reports
2. The number and nature of problems encountered, and the vendor's promptness in resolving them
3. Number of items the vendor was unable to provide

Duration will depend on how much time and effort is considered appropriate. Any process can be analyzed in microscopic detail, but that level of attention is probably not necessary unless the entire performance of the vendor seems unsatisfactory.

Conclusion

Selecting the best vendor to handle the library's approval plans, serials, databases, and other services is only part of the RFP process. If the award goes to a vendor not currently under contract with the library, the library must plan and follow up on the transfer. Further, librarians must ensure that the vendor is fulfilling its obligations to the library by conducting periodic vendor performance evaluations and by working with the vendor to correct any deficiencies.

Schedules and Forms for the RFP Process

The schedules, forms, and samples presented in this appendix are the following:

1. Sample Timeline for an RFP Process (Academic Year)
2. Sample Cover Letter
3. Model Language for an RFP

    Model Language for Assessing Common Vendor Capabilities

    Model Language for Determining Overall Cost Considerations

    Model Task Force Evaluation of Proposals

4. Sample Questions for Vendor References
5. Sample Vendor Evaluation Form
6. Sample Letter of Justification of Award

Sample Timeline for an RFP Process (Academic Year)

The timeline can be modified to suit other types of schedules, as needed.

October through mid-November

- Appoint RFP Task Force, elect chair (if chair is not already designated)
- Meet with purchasing agent to determine institutional requirements
- Have discussions and conduct research (if needed) on RFP requirements for library
- Select vendors to receive the RFP, arrange on-site visits (if desired)

Mid-November through mid-January

- Write RFP
- Make RFP available for review and comment by other library employees (if appropriate)

Early February

- Send RFP to purchasing agent for review
- Purchasing agent reviews RFP, makes any needed changes, specifies date by which vendor responses are due, and sends it to all appropriate vendors

Mid-February through April

- Vendors have a specified number of days (typically, 30-45 days depending upon delivery time) to respond to the RFP

■ RFP Task Force chair (or designate) answers any vendor questions (if appropriate/allowed by purchasing department)

April

■ Purchasing department receives all proposals, officially opens them, and forwards them to the library for review and selection

■ RFP Task Force evaluates vendor proposals and calls or emails vendor references

■ RFP Task Force reviews and tabulates evaluation forms, discusses reference answers, and selects a vendor

■ RFP Task Force provides recommendation, justification, and all supporting documentation and materials to purchasing agent

May

■ Purchasing department awards vendor contract to successful vendor

■ Purchasing department notifies all vendors of award decision

July

■ New vendor contract(s) begins

■ Library begins implementation process

Sample Cover Letter

To: Vendor

From: Library

Subject: Request for Proposal for [materials or services]
         Purchasing Department Number [123]

This Request for Proposal (RFP) is to supply [specify materials or services] for the library [name]. If your organization chooses to submit a proposal, please note that it must be received by the purchasing department, [contact name, street address, email address, phone number] by [time and date]. The format of the response must be [print or electronic]. Please provide [X] copies of your proposal and [Y] copies of any exhibits.

The library requires three client references from libraries similar to itself in size and purpose. If possible, one of these libraries should have recently transferred its account to your company. If possible, one of these libraries should have the [name of your ILS] integrated library system. Please provide the name of the person to contact, along with their phone number, email, and street address.

This service will take effect on [date]. The contract will be valid for [x] years, with the option of [z] renewals of [y] years each. Such extensions, if granted, will be by the mutual consent of both parties, and will be based upon the criteria set forth in this proposal and contingent on the availability of funding. The library anticipates spending approximately $[X] dollars annually on this service. These amounts should not be considered as a commitment to purchase but are intended to provide the vendor with an estimated value. The library reserves the right to increase or decrease expenditures as its needs and funding changes determine.

All vendor responses will be evaluated by the library's RFP Task Force and reviewed by the library director and the Purchasing Department. The library reserves the right to use the services of two or more vendors if it deems the vendors' services to be of overall equal value. The vendor should submit its best-and-final pricing offer in its proposal and indicate if there are separate offers for all versus parts of the library's account. (*Splitting an account is more common for large serials accounts than for specialized approval plans; omit this sentence if it is not appropriate.*) The library is not obligated to award the contract based only on lowest price considerations. Responses that do not provide all required information will be eliminated from consideration. Please do not minimize the importance of responding to all questions.

The vendor has the sole responsibility to inquire about any sections of the RFP that it considers unclear. [Include contact information for the purchasing department individual handling the account, the chair of the library's RFP Task Force and an additional member of the RFP Task Force, and a library systems/technical contact. Include names, street addresses, phone numbers, fax numbers and e-mail addresses.]

Background Information

[Describe the library and the parent organization: clientele, programs, and size and strength of its collections; operating budget; staff size; and appropriate information about its technical requirements. Include integrated library system, bibliographic utility used, consortia memberships, and any other information that will assist the vendor.]

Evaluation Factors

The weighted point system to be used to determine the appropriate vendor will include, but not be limited to, the following:

Company Data	10%
Coverage Provided	30%
Customer Service	40%
Overall Cost Considerations	20%

Model Language for an RFP

This section lists common elements of the RFP and describes how to address them.

Cover Letter

Include the cover letter, as described in the sample cover letter in this appendix.

General Requirements

This section outlines what the library is purchasing from the vendor such as an approval plan or a serials account.

Required Capabilities

This section will be relatively small and will contain only those elements that the vendor must provide or be eliminated from consideration. For example, you might require that an approval plan vendor be able to transmit electronically bibliographic records for your approval shipments that you could load into your integrated library system or that a serials vendor is able to provide both print and electronic formats. These required elements are the core of the project.

Company Background

1. Describe your company. How long have you been in business? How large is the company? How many libraries similar to this library are customers of your company? What are the backgrounds of the personnel who would be working with the library?

2. What is the financial condition of the company? Please provide a financial report or documentation describing the financial solvency of the company.

3. How would the library's account be handled? Would there be an assigned representative responsible for communication with the library?

Model Language for Assessing Common Vendor Capabilities

The following types of questions are often posed in the body of the RFP.

Electronic or Computer-based Services

1. Do you have an online database of the books or serials you provide? Please describe the coverage, access and features.
2. Can your database be used by the library to order or claim materials? Does it have the capability to create on-demand management reports?

Customer Service

1. How will the vendor communicate with the library?
2. What is the expected response time in which questions from the library receive a response?
3. Does the vendor have e-mail discussion lists or online tutorials for training?

Questions for Approval Plans

1. What is your coverage (geographic, subject, format)? What materials are excluded?
2. How does your company profile materials for the library? Please provide examples of your thesaurus and other profiling tools. How is reprofiling done? Are there limits on the amount of reprofiling that can be requested by the library?
3. Describe your database of titles. Please provide the library with trial online access to the database.
4. What value-added services do you provide, such as bibliographic records, shelf-ready processing, management reports, etc?
5. How do you handle simultaneous publication in multiple formats (hardbound, paperback, electronic, audio)?
6. What return rate is considered acceptable?

Questions for a Serials Account

1. What is your coverage (geographic, subject, format)? What materials do you exclude?
2. How do you handle memberships, electronic journals, electronic journal packages and databases?
3. Describe your database of titles. Please provide the library with trial online access to the database.
4. What value-added services do you provide, such as bibliographic records, shelf-ready processing, management reports, etc?

Questions for a Database Account

1. What is your coverage for the database? For example, subjects, journal titles, media, electronic resources, etc.
2. How frequently is the database updated?
3. How are usage statistics provided?
4. Can the library tailor the appearance of the database by using an administrative module?
5. Are bibliographic records provided for the titles of the books or journals included in the database?

Model Language for Determining Overall Cost Considerations

1. Please provide a complete list of your pricing. Include all special charges, such as those for rush orders. Will the charges vary depending upon the size and mix of the library's account? If so, please describe the options.
2. Are discounts available if the library prepays or establishes a deposit account? Please provide exact details.
3. Are there charges for value-added services, such as enhanced bibliographic records? Please list all possible costs.
4. If you are an international company, is the library billed in U.S. dollars? If not, how is the conversion/exchange rate handled?

Model for Task Force Evaluation of Proposals

The criteria will depend upon the nature of the RFP and the library's priorities. Criteria correspond to the sections of the RFP. The library will establish the weighting factors in consultation with the purchasing agent. For example:

Company Data	10%
Coverage Provided	30%
Customer Service	40%
Overall Cost Considerations	20%

Sample Questions
for Vendor References

These questions can be directed to libraries that the vendor gives as references when responding to the RFP. You can add other questions that reflect your library's requirements.

1. How long has your library used this vendor? In what capacity?

2. What does vendor X do well? Are there areas of that need improvement?

3. Has your library ever experienced problems with vendor X? If so, how were the problems discovered? How were they handled?

4. What is your experience with vendor X's online system? Is it well-organized and easy to use?

5. What is your experience with vendor X's website? Is it well-organized and easy to use?

6. Does vendor X communicate with your library in a timely and effective way? Through email, phone, on-site visits, and other means?

   - Does vendor X provide on-site training for your staff? Online training? Is it helpful?

   - If you recently transferred your account to vendor X, what assistance did they provide? Was it helpful? What went well? What needed improvement?

   - If you had it to do over again, would you select this vendor? Why or why not?

   - Is there anything you would like to add?

Sample Vendor Evaluation Form

The vendor evaluation form lists the evaluation criteria and the percentages specified for each criterion in the library's RFP. The following paragraphs show one way to organize the vendor evaluation form.

Vendor Name: _____

Evaluator Name: _____ Date: _____

Company Data, 10%

    Percentage Score (0-10%): _____

    Why did you assign this percentage score: _____

    _____

Coverage Provided (profiling and title selection for approval plans; geographic coverage, format specialization, etc., for serials) 30%

    Percentage Score (0-30%): _____

    Why did you assign this percentage score: _____

    _____

Customer Service, 40%

    Percentage Score (0-40%) _____

    Why did you assign this percentage score: _____

    _____

Overall Cost Considerations (discount or service charge, prepayment, shipping charges, etc.), 20%

    Percentage Score (0-20%) _____

    Why did you assign this percentage score: _____

    _____

Total points awarded: _____

Over all justification and comments: _____

_____

Sample Letter of Justification of Award

TO: Joe Doe, Procurement Agent III, Purchasing Department

FROM: Jane Smith, Library RFP Task Force Chair

SUBJECT: RFP #123 for domestic approval plan

The Library conducted RFP #123 for a domestic approval plan. The RFP Task Force consisted of six members [name them]. Responses were received from three companies [name them]. The task force, in consultation with the Library Director [name him/her] recommends that the approval plan contract be awarded to Vendor Y.

The following table shows the criteria used to rank the vendors.

Criterion	Percentage Assigned
Company Data	10
Coverage Provided	30
Customer Service	40
Overall Cost Considerations	20
Total for all criteria	100

The following table shows the points assigned to the three vendors during the proposal evaluation.

Criterion	Vendor X (%)	Vendor Y (%)	Vendor Z (%)
Company Data	7	9	6
Coverage Provided	25	28	21
Customer Service	34	38	30
Overall Cost Considerations	17	17	18
Total	83	92	75

Vendor Z scored the lowest of the respondents, with 75%. They did not demonstrate the ability to provide the variety of materials desired, and their financial statement contained several omissions in areas stipulated in the RFP requirements. Although they offered a deeper discount than the other vendors, this factor alone did not compensate for their weaknesses in other areas.

Vendor X and Vendor Y are comparable in terms of overall cost considerations, and their discounts are identical. However, Vendor Y is superior in the remaining categories, notably in the heaviest-weighted category, customer service. In that area, Vendor X's references were not as positive as Vendor Y's.

Enclosed are the original evaluation forms from each member of the RFP Task Force, along with email responses and transcripts of the calls made to references for each vendor.

Please notify me as soon as your review of the documentation is complete and the award is made. Thank you for your assistance.

The Library RFP Process: A Task-Based View

Planning	*Writing*
• **Constructing a timeline** • **Selecting an RFP Task Force** • **Etc.** • **Etc.**	• **Preparing the cover letter** • **Establishing . . .** • **Etc.**

Periods
- Display/print list of periods
- Add or delete periods
- Modify duration or start date
- Modify task sequence

Schedule subdivision water delivery
- Schedule pickup of signup sheets
- Display or update task status for current period
- Set up subdivision for the current period
- Pull-in subdivision members and durations
- Review or adjust current orders in Request Manager
- Display subdivision sequence
- Accept a schedule
- Send a schedule
- Display or print hangback sheets or special run sheets

- Schedule special runs/ exceptions
- Special a subdivision
- Change subdivision schedule after a Send

Evaluation/Awards

- Reviewing proposals . . .
- Contacting vendor references
- Completing vendor evaluation forms . . .

Contract Inplementation and Post-Award Evaluation

- **Implementing the contract**
- **Performing the initial follow-up**
- **Evaluating vendor performance post-award**
- Create or modify global parameters
- Create or modify annual parameters
- Create or modify transaction types
- Create or modify season types

- Maintain subdivision information
- Display/print list of subdivisions
- Maintain subdivision assignments

- Maintain account and ditch information
- Maintain ditch assignments
- Maintain account assignments.
- View accounts and ditches in physical or delivery sequence
- Maintain physical sequence
- Maintain delivery sequence

GLOSSARY

Annual value of the award: The dollar amount the library projects that it will spend annually with the vendor. This amount should be included in the cover letter for the RFP.

Approval plan: Approval plans provide books matched to a profile of subjects, publishers, formats, etc. desired by the library.

Bibliographic utilities: Entities such as OCLC that provide bibliographic and cataloging records to libraries for their online public access catalogs (OPACs).

Boilerplate: Sections of the cover letter that can be reused from one RFP to another.

Competitive procurement process: A bidding and award process, often state-mandated, that affords each vendor equal opportunity to state its ability to supply a product or service through a proposal or bidding process. No vendor is given special advantage, and the process is most often accomplished through an RFP, RFI, or RFQ or bid.

Computer-based services: Computerized services that the library may seek from a vendor, including system interfaces and capabilities and electronic services such as electronic ordering, claiming, management reports, and vendor inventory.

Contract: A legal, written agreement between the library or parent institution and the vendor clearly stating the requirements and specifications of the agreement. Often, the library's RFP, with the vendor's response and the award letter, will constitute the contract.

Contract award letter: A letter sent to the successful vendor, generally sent by the institution's purchasing agent at the conclusion of the RFP process.

Cover letter: A letter accompanying the RFP, often part of the administrative section, that summarizes for the vendor the types of materials and services that the RFP covers. In some cases, this portion of the RFP may also include the estimated dollar value of the contract, the timeframe and format in which the vendor must respond, a description of the library and its parent organizations, contact names, and the criteria to be used to evaluate the vendor's response.

Debarment: The legal exclusion of a vendor from consideration under an RFP for a valid reason.

Disclaimer: The exclusion of some part of an RFP, if certain conditions arise. For example, a disclaimer against the annual dollar value of the award means that the contract amount could be reduced if the library's budget is reduced.

Discount: Reductions in the list price of materials, offered by vendors to publishers. Although these discounts depend upon the discounts offered by individual publishers, such discounts are often offered at a set rate for all library purchases if the range of materials to be bought is fairly broad.

Evaluation criteria: Standards for evaluating the vendor responses to the RFP, reflecting the needs and concerns of the library. Each criterion should be assigned a weight and number of possible points so that the vendor will understand the factors by which its response will be judged.

General terms and conditions: Contract stipulations regarding the general conduct and possible longevity of the contract. The stipulations typically include criteria and conditions for the acceptance and rejection of products and services; addresses where notices can be sent; assignment of the contract; multiple awards; cancellation, changes, and alterations after the award; conflict of interest clauses; discounts, requirements of financial statement, references required, governing law, indemnification and insurance, inspections, patent and copyright indemnity, penalties, proposed negotiation rules, termination and delays, warranties, and equal opportunity and affirmative action statements. These are sometimes found in the cover letter or may be found in other introductory sections.

Instructions to vendors: Detailed directions to vendors on practical matters related to the RFP including clarifications, addenda, failure to respond, late submission, rejection of offers, etc. The instructions usually include a detailed statement of conflict of interest and debarment. These are usually found in the cover letter.

Integrated library system (ILS): A system in which components work together to perform library functions such as ordering, cataloging, circulation, etc.

Library contact: Generally the Chair of the RFP Task Force whom the vendor may contact regarding questions about the RFP.

Minority vendor: A business owned by a member of an ethnic or racial minority. Some states have regulations designed to ensure that minority-owned businesses receive either equal or preferential consideration when competing for an RFP.

Non-disclosure: Vendors may designate some portion of their responses (typically financial data) as confidential. Such information is made available only to members of the RFP Task Force and the purchasing agent.

Non-prejudicial language: Language that is unbiased, impartial, and non-discriminatory. The RFP must be free from prejudicial language that unfairly favors one vendor over another.

Prepayment: A payment made for an item prior to its being delivered to the library. This practice is especially common for serials.

Procurement code: A set of legal rules or statutes for acquiring products or services, typically issued by a state, county, or local government or an institution.

Profile: A document that sets forth specifications and guidelines for the type of books a vendor should supply to the library.

The profile may include subject specifications, publishers to exclude, duplication controls, and selection preferences based on country of origin, format, binding, and other factors.

Purchasing agent: The person assigned to the library to oversee and facilitate the RFP process; to ensure that institutional, state, and federal regulations are followed; and to process the contract award documents.

Purchasing department: The department in the parent institution that is charged with overseeing the competitive procurement process.

Recommendation document: A document provided by the RFP Task Force to the library director and to the purchasing agent to recommending a vendor to receive the award. The recommendation document should include a list of all vendors submitting proposals, the evaluation criteria and scores for each vendor, the recommendation, and the reasons why the recommendation is made.

Recommendation form: The form used by the RFP Task Force to score each vendor's response.

References: Libraries whose names the vendor has submitted to provide opinions of the vendor's performance and other information about the vendor.

Request for information (RFI): The RFI asks for general information regarding a vendor's services. It does not state library requirements. RFIs are often valuable tools for a library to determine what it requires prior to writing an RFP.

Request for proposal (RFP): The RFP is as a process as well as a document. As a process, it provides an objective method for a library to state its requirements, evaluate vendor proposals, and justify its award decision. As a document, it includes the library's requirements, additional services the library would like to consider, and the steps to be followed for vendors who wish to submit proposals to handle the library's account(s).

Request for quotation (or Quote): When using an RFQ, awards are based entirely on the lowest-price bid for a product or service. This process is best suited to purchase of products rather than services.

Service charge: A charge above the list cost of a title by a vendor for service, usually associated with serials accounts. The amount will depend on the size and mix of the library's account.

Shelf-ready materials: Books or other library materials that are already processed (cataloged, labeled, property-stamped, etc.) by the vendor and ready to be shelved by the library.

Timeline: A document displaying the projected activities involved in the RFP process in the order of their occurrence, with corresponding dates for completing hose activities. It should be a dynamic document, open to modification, especially during initial meetings with the purchasing agent and the RFP Task Force.

Transfer process: The transfer of titles in a given category (for example, domestic standing orders or European periodicals) from one or more vendors to one or more different vendors.

Value-added service: A service that enhances a basic product, thus adding value to it (for example, adding table of contents notes to a cataloging record).

Vendor evaluation: A project conducted to judge vendor performance—how well the vendor met the conditions of its contract with the library.

Vendor performance data: Data used in vendor evaluation projects, including such elements as fulfillment times, rate of returns for approval plans, and claims response time.

PRINT AND ONLINE PUBLICATIONS

Anderson, Rick. *Buying and Contracting for Resources and Services: A How-to-do-it Manual for Librarians* (New York: Neal-Schuman Publishers, Inc., 2004).

Clegg, Helen and Susan Montgomery. "How to Write an RFP for Information Producers." *Information Outlook* 10, no. 6 (2006): 23–33.

Fowler, Mark W. "How to Bring Sanity to Insane RFPs." *AIIM E-Doc Magazine* 18, no. 2 (2004): 44–46.

Fria, Rick. *Successful RFPs in Construction: Managing the Request for Proposal Process* (New York: McGraw Hill, 2005).

"Guidelines for Technical Issues in Request for Proposal Requirements and Contract Negotiations." *Information Technology and Libraries* 18, no. 3 (1999): 164–68, www.library.yale.edu/consortia/techreq.html. (accessed December. 19, 2006).

Hodgson, Cynthia. *The RFP Writer's Guide to Standards for Library Systems* (Bethesda, Md.: National Information Standards Organization, 2002), www.niso.com (accessed May 10, 2007).

Kendall, Mark. "Issues in Vendor-Library Relations: The RFP Process—a Book Vendor's Musings." *Against the Grain* 14, no. 6 (2002/2003): 82–83.

Kuhn, Maria. "Biz of Acq: How to Select a Vendor for an Approval Plan." *Against the Grain* 18, no 1 (2006): 51–52.

Porter-Roth, Bud. *Request for Proposal: a Guide to Effective RFP Development* (Boston: Addison-Wesley, 2002).

Porter-Roth, Bud. *RFP Guidelines for an Enterprise Content Management System: an AIIM User Guide* (Silver Spring, Md.: AIIM International, 2004).

Rumph, Virginia A. "Vendor Selection Using the RFP Process—Is It for You?—One Library's Experience" *Indiana Libraries* 20, no. 1 (2001): 26–28.

Schachter, Debbie. "How to Manage the RRP Process." *Information Outlook* 8, no. 1 (2004): 10–12.

Stowe, Melinda. "To RFP or Not to RFP: That is the Question." *Journal of Library Administration* 26, nos. 3 and 4 (1999): 53–74.

Stuthard, Brenda. "Writing the Fulfillment RFP." *CM/Circulation Management* 17, no. 8 (2002): 32–37.

Waller, Nicole. "Model RFP for Integrated Library System Products: Special Issue." *Library Technology Reports* 39, no. 4 (2003), 5–66.

Wilkinson, Frances C. and Connie Capers Thorson. *The RFP Process: Effective Management of the Acquisition of Library Materials* (Englewood, Colo.: Libraries Unlimited, Inc., 1998).

RECOMMENDED READING

Webography

Many libraries post their RFPs on the Internet. Because these documents change frequently, we will not list specific addresses for RFPs. Instead, we recommend that you use a Web browser and the search terms "libraries" and "rfp" to find current examples.

Selected Electronic Discussion Lists

Electronic discussion lists are a means for colleagues to exchange information and ask questions about areas of librarianship. The lists described here may be helpful when you are preparing an RFP.

Acqnet   A medium for acquisitions librarians and others interested in acquisitions work to exchange information, ideas, and solutions. http://www.acqweb.org/acqnet.html

Colldv-l   For collection development librarians and those interested in that field. http://infomotions.com/serials/colldv-l

Liblicense-l   Focused on the topic of electronic content licensing for academic and research librarians. http://www.library .yale.edu/~llicense/ mailing-list.shtml

Serialst   For most aspects of serials librarianship and serials processing. http://www.uvm.edu/~bmaclenn/serialst.html

Selected Web Sites

AIIM　The Enterprise Content Management Association. http://www.aiim.org.

Information about document and record management, including resources for preparing RFPs.

Non-profit Guides　Grant-writing Tools for Non-profit Organizations. http://www.npguides.org.

Information about preparing grant applications and RFPs.

Techsoup　The Technology Place for Nonprofits. http://www.techsoup.org/index.cfm Information about the RFP process.

3149 037

Printed in the United States
125361LV00003B/343-429/P